Ultimate FACTIVITY Collection

DINOSAURS

Create your own book about the prehistoric world

DK

LONDON, NEW YORK, MUNICH,
MELBOURNE, AND DELHI

Editor James Mitchem
US Editor Margaret Parrish
Senior Designer Clare Shedden
Designers Ria Holland, Yumiko Tahata
Design Assistance Charlotte Bull, Glenda Fisher,
Elaine Hewson, Charlotte Johnson
Editorial Assistance Ellie de Rose
Consultant Darren Naish
Jacket Designers Ria Holland, Rosie Levine, Natasha Rees
Illustrators Helen Dodsworth, Chris Howker, Barney Ibbotson, Jake McDonald
Pre-Production Producer Sarah Isle
Senior Producer Alex Bell
Creative Technical Support Sonia Charbonnier
Managing Editor Penny Smith
Senior Managing Art Editor Marianne Markham
Publisher Mary Ling
Creative Director Jane Bull

First American Edition, 2014
Published in the United States by DK Publishing
4th floor, 345 Hudson Street, New York, New York 10014

14 15 16 17 18   10 9 8 7 6 5 4 3 2 1
001–196311–07/14

A catalog record for this book is available from the Library of Congress.
ISBN: 978-1-4654-1656-8

DK books are available at special discounts when purchased in bulk for sales
promotions, premiums, fund-raising, or educational use. For details, contact: DK Publishing
Special Markets, 345 Hudson Street, New York, New York 10014 or SpecialSales@dk.com.

Printed and bound in China by L. Rex Printing Co., Ltd.
Discover more at **www.dk.com**

The prehistoric world

Long ago, before humans even existed, amazing creatures called dinosaurs roamed the Earth. These incredible reptiles are one of history's greatest treasures.

Page _____

Page _____

FIND

these pictures on pages 4–17 and write the page numbers in the boxes.

Page _____

Page _____

Page _____

Page _____

Don't forget to put your stickers in first.

2

MATCH

the name of each dinosaur with its meaning by studying the clues.

What do these names mean?

- Tyrannosaurus rex
- Stegosaurus
- Gallimimus
- Oviraptor
- Velociraptor
- Triceratops

1 Roof lizard

"Saurus" means lizard.

2 Egg thief

"Ovi" means egg in Latin.

3 Chicken mimic

I wonder what raptor means...

4 Speedy thief

$

5 Three-horned face

Psst. "Tri" means three.

6 Tyrant lizard king

What did they look like?

Big, small, and everything in between, dinosaurs came in all shapes and sizes. Do you think you can draw them accurately?

STEGOSAURUS

- Walked on all fours, low to the ground.
- Had short front legs and longer back legs with hooflike toes.
- A double row of diamond-shaped plates ran down its neck, back, and long tail.
- Its head was narrow with a beaklike mouth.

SIZE GUIDE

TRICERATOPS

- Walked on all fours with short, thick legs.
- Had a large, bony crest that looked like a collar covering its skull.
- Had two large horns above its eyes and a smaller one by its nose.
- It had a rhinolike body.

SIZE GUIDE

DRAW

each dinosaur in the frames by using the clues as a guide, but be creative!

EORAPTOR

- Walked and ran on its strong back legs.
- It wasn't much bigger than a chicken, but had a large head.
- Had sharp claws.

SIZE GUIDE

BRACHIOSAURUS

- Its gigantic body was supported by thick, strong legs.
- A very long neck helped it reach treetops for food.
- It had a very long and thick tail.
- Its head was small for its size, with a bump on top.

SIZE GUIDE

Leg bone

Can you find all these dinosaurs in this book?

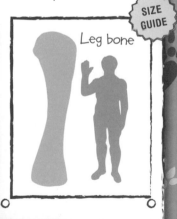

The Mesozoic Era

Dinosaurs are one of the most successful creatures ever to exist. They ruled the Earth for about 186 million years during a time called the Mesozoic Era.

COLOR the dinosaurs and pterosaurs for all three periods of the Mesozoic Era.

The Mesozoic Era was split up into three periods.

Pangaea

At the start of the Mesozoic Era, the Earth's continents were all joined together into one big land mass called **Pangaea** (All Earth). Over millions of years they broke up to form the continents we know today.

TRUE OR FALSE? T. REX LIVED CLOSER IN TIME TO HUMANS THAN IT DID TO EARLY DINOSAURS.

Herrerasaurus

Coelophysis

Lesothosaurus

Mussaurus

The Triassic
251–200 million years ago

Oviraptor

Archaeopteryx

Pterodactylus

Brachiosaurus

Tyrannosaurus rex

Pachycephalosaurus

Stegosaurus

Triceratops

Iguanodon

Spinosaurus

Velociraptor

The Cretaceous
145–65 million years ago

The Jurassic
200–145 million years ago

Humans don't arrive for millions of years!

Triassic
period

Find the stickers by color and shape

The first dinosaurs

Plateosaurus

PLATE-ee-oh-SORE-us

At 25ft (8m) long, Plateosaurus was one of the biggest dinosaurs from the Triassic.

Herrerasaurus

Her-RARE-uh-SORE-us

This early meat-eater lived 228 million years ago, but was only discovered in 1961CE.

Thecodontosaurus

THEE-co-DON-toe-SORE-us

One of the first dinosaurs to be discovered, its name means "socket-tooth lizard."

Pisanosaurus

PIE-san-uh-SORE-us

At only 3ft (1m) long, Pisanosaurus was the first known "bird-hipped" dinosaur.

Eoraptor

EE-oh-rap-tor

About the size of a fox, Eoraptor used its sharp claws and teeth to help catch its prey.

STICK

the stickers next to the descriptions and fill the rest of the scene with dinosaurs.

8

The first period in the Mesozoic Era was called the Triassic. It spanned from 251–200 million years ago and was the time when the first dinosaurs emerged.

Dinosaurs weren't very big during the Triassic period.

TRUE OR FALSE?
THE DINOSAUR STEGOSAURUS LIVED DURING THE TRIASSIC PERIOD.

Facts about...

Earth
The planet looked very different during the Triassic. Because it was so much **hotter and drier**, there weren't many plants, and most of the land was covered in desert.

Jurassic period

During the Jurassic period the planet grew a lot cooler. This allowed more trees and plants to grow, and was one of the reasons so many new species of dinosaur emerged.

SPOT the five differences between the two pictures of the sauropods.

Sauropods like me are the biggest creatures ever to walk on land!

Brachiosaurus, one of the largest sauropods, grew up to 75ft (23m) long!

Sauropods

Among the dinosaurs to emerge during the Jurassic were the Sauropods. These giants had **long tails and necks**, which helped them reach leaves to eat from the tops of tall trees.

Games

Cretaceous period

The Cretaceous lasted around 80 million years, and by the time it was over the Earth had become a very different place from the early days of the Triassic.

STICK

the stickers of Earth in the circles, then add dinosaur stickers to the continents.

Add the Triassic world sticker here.

Triassic Earth

Toward the end of the Triassic, the supercontinent Pangaea began to break up into several smaller landmasses.

Add the Jurassic world sticker here.

Jurassic Earth

The newly formed continents drifted apart during the Jurassic, creating large shallow seas.

Pentaceratops

Titanosaurus

Giganotosaurus

Cretaceous Earth

During the Cretaceous, the supercontinent Pangaea split apart farther, and the Earth's continents began to look more like they do today.

I wonder what the world was like during the Cretaceous period.

Modern Earth

Today the Earth is divided into seven continents. They're still moving—it just happens so slowly that it's hard to tell.

Gallimimus

Spinosaurus

Minmi

I lived in what is now North America. Can you tell where that was?

Different types of dinosaur

Which type am I?

Dinosaurs

Saurischians
One type of dinosaur, saurischians, was called "lizard-hipped."

An example of a saurischian's hip.

Ornithischians
The other type, ornithischians, was known as "bird-hipped."

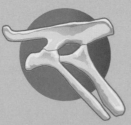

An example of an ornithischian's hip.

Theropods
(THERRO-pods)
A group of meat-eaters that **walked on two legs**, theropods had strong jaws and curved teeth to help them chew meat.

Sauropodomorphs
(SORE-oh-POD-oh-morfs)
Famous for their **long necks and tails**, these plant-eaters were the biggest animals ever to walk the Earth.

Thyreophorans
(THIGH-ree-OFF-oh-rans)
These plant-eaters are known for their impressive **armored plates** and spikes.

Ornithopods
(OR-nith-oh-pods)
A very common group of dinosaur, ornithopods reached for food with their beaks and cropping teeth.

Marginocephalians
(MAR-jee-no-sa-FAY-lee-ans)
With distinctive **frills and horns**, this group of plant-eater was common during the Cretaceous period.

Dinosaurs came in all shapes and sizes, but there were only two main types (based on the hip bones). These dinosaurs could then be split up into five smaller groups.

FOLLOW the lines and write down which type of dinosaur each one is.

Ouranosaurus

I am an _

Huayangosaurus

I am a _

Argentinosaurus

I am a _

Triceratops

I am a _

Wow, these are long names!

Timimus

I am a _

Games

15

Sticker gallery

Allosaurus
This predator from the Jurassic had razor-sharp teeth.

Pentaceratops
The spiked horns on its head helped it defend itself.

Edmontonia
It was covered in dagger-like armored spikes.

Sauropods
These giants often lived by rivers and coasts.

STICK
the correct stickers for each frame in the right place.

Corythosaurus
The crest on its head could have been used to "talk" to its herd.

DRAW your favorite dinosaur and write its name in the box.

Age of the dinosaurs

The dinosaurs as we think of them became extinct 65 million years ago, but to this day they fascinate us. How many of these facts about dinosaurs did you know?

Page _____

Page _____

Page _____

FIND these pictures on pages 20–33 and write the page numbers in the boxes.

Page _____

Page _____

Page _____

Don't forget to put your stickers in first.

18

STICK

the sticker that matches each creature and read the facts about each one.

1 Quetzalcoatlus

With a massive wingspan 39ft (12m) across, Quetzalcoatlus was the largest creature ever to fly.

39ft

2 Spinosaurus

It was actually Spinosaurus, not Tyrannosaurus rex, who was the biggest meat-eater ever to walk the Earth.

3 Archaeopteryx

About the same size as a modern raven, Archaeopteryx was the first known bird.

4 Diplodocus

The gigantic sauropod Diplodocus could grow to 115ft (35m) long, and its whiplike tail contained about 80 bones.

Around **80** bones

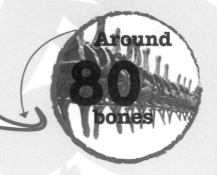

Solid bone dome!

6 Pachycephalosaurus

This plant-eater had a solid dome on its head that it would use like a battering ram to fight off enemies and rivals.

5 Suchomimus

This dinosaur had a long snout and claws, which were useful for catching fish.

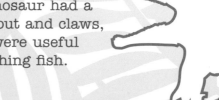

Quizzes

19

Flying high with
pterosaurs

While dinosaurs ruled the land, pterosaurs owned the sky. These flying reptiles usually had hollow bones and small bodies, but could have wingspans up to 36ft (11m).

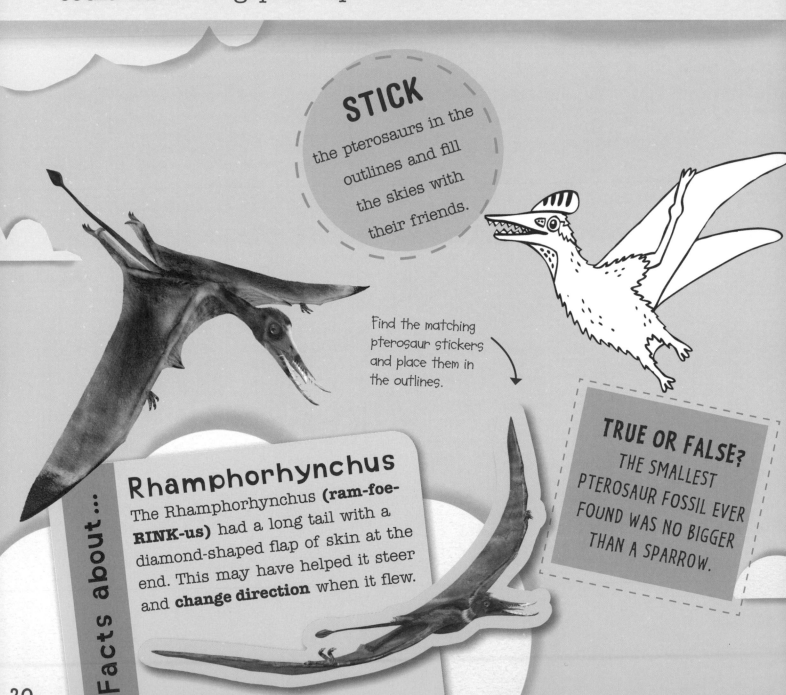

STICK the pterosaurs in the outlines and fill the skies with their friends.

Find the matching pterosaur stickers and place them in the outlines.

Facts about...

Rhamphorhynchus
The Rhamphorhynchus (**ram-foe-RINK-us**) had a long tail with a diamond-shaped flap of skin at the end. This may have helped it steer and **change direction** when it flew.

TRUE OR FALSE?
THE SMALLEST PTEROSAUR FOSSIL EVER FOUND WAS NO BIGGER THAN A SPARROW.

Facts about...

Dimorphodon

Its unusually large head was about a third of its body length and contained two types of teeth that were perfect for trapping prey.

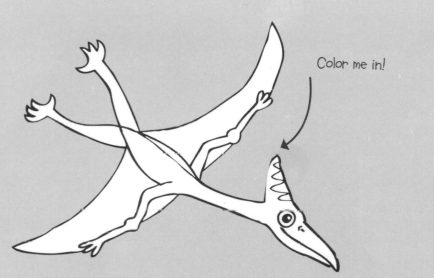

Color me in!

Facts about...

Pteranodon

This pterosaur was given its name (pteranodon means "**wing without tooth**") after fossil collectors discovered it had **no teeth** at all.

Facts about...

Pterodactylus

One of the best-known pterosaurs, it had a short tail and slender neck, and its wings were covered in a leathery material that helped it **fly quickly**.

The mixed-up scrap book

Oops! Someone has mixed up the labels in the dinosaur scrapbook. Can you use the clues on the tags to figure out which is which?

Suchomimus
- Had a narrow hump along its back.
- Its head looked a little like a crocodile's.
- Walked on its hind legs.
- Had a long, slender skull.

Giganotosaurus
- Had short forearms with sharp claws.
- A relative of T. rex.
- Walked on strong hind legs.
- Had razor-sharp teeth.

Dimorphodon
- Had a large head and beak.
- Its tail was fairly thin.
- Is was actually a pterosaur, not a dinosaur.
- Its wings were made of skin.

Mamenchisaurus
- Walked on four legs.
- Was a herbivore.
- Had one of the longest necks of any animal in history.
- Had a strong thick hide.

1

Pentaceratops
- Was a herbivore.
- Walked on four legs.
- Had a large beak.
- Used its horns for defense.
- Had a large, armored skull.

2

3

Are you a dino BRAINBOX or a dino DUNCE?

MATCH the descriptions to each dinosaur and write their names in the boxes.

5

4

23

2

1

3

STICK the marine reptiles in the right spot, then match them to the descriptions.

Under the sea

Dinosaurs were land-based creatures, but during the time they walked the land, other creatures, called marine reptiles, lurked beneath the ocean waves.

Facts about... Pliosaurus

This giant beast (seen below) grew up to 40ft (12m) long and was one of the deadliest marine reptiles of all time. Until 2012, it was referred to as **"Predator X."**

4

Ichthyosaurus
• Had a small, slim snout.
• Its body was shaped a bit like a dolphin's.
• Had fairly large eyes for its size.

Metriorhynchus
• It looked a little like a prehistoric crocodile.
• Had a long, powerful tail with a large fin at the back.

Elasmosaurus
• Its neck was as long as its entire body.
• Its head was very small compared to its body.
• Had four large flippers.

Lariosaurus
• It had paddles instead of front legs, with claws at the back.
• Its tail was thin, with no fin at the back.

Write the number for each answer here.

25

Dino sticker puzzles

STICK
the stickers onto the grids to match the dinosaur pictures.

Dinosaurs come in all shapes and sizes. How well do you think you can tell them apart? Find out with these sticker puzzles.

TRUE OR FALSE?
SALTASAURUS MEANS SALT-EATING LIZARD.

Saltasaurus

Facts about...

This herbivore from the Late Cretaceous was one of the last of the dinosaurs. It grazed on plants and had a **thick hide** that helped to protect it from predators.

Saltasaurus

Spinosaurus

How big?

It may not be as famous as T. rex, but Spinosaurus was the **largest predator** to walk on land. It could grow to 60ft (18m) in length.

Spinosaurus

Facts about...

This massive predator from the Late Cretaceous was best known for the large **sail-like spine** on its back. Spinosaurus feasted on fish, birds, turtles, and other dinosaurs.

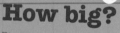

27

A-**maze**-ing escape!

Life could be hard for a dinosaur. Some of them, such as Tenontosaurus, couldn't easily defend themselves against attackers, and hungry predators could be lurking around every corner!

START

Color me in

DRAW

a safe route through the maze, then check the box by each predator you spot.

Color me in

I only eat plants, but these dinosaurs are scary!

Tenontosaurus
ten-NON-toe-SORE-us

END

Good job! But now I'm hungry...

How do you say the names of these dinosaurs?

Hungry predators

Tyrannosaurus rex
TIE-ran-oh-SORE-us
The king of dinosaurs, and maybe the most fearsome predator of all.

Giganotosaurus
gig-AN-oh-toe-SORE-rus
A relative of T. rex that lived about 25 million years earlier.

Utahraptor
YOU-tah-RAP-tor
Most famous for its deadly claws, it was a fierce hunter.

Carnotaurus
CAR-no-TORE-us
A fairly large predator with thick horns above its eyes.

Deinonychus
dye-NON-ee-cuss
A small, but deadly pack hunter from the Cretaceous period.

Spinosaurus
SPINE-oh-SORE-us
The largest predator ever to walk the Earth.

Games

How many dinosaurs?

Do you have a keen eye? There are three species of dinosaur on these pages. How many of each type can you spot?

WRITE down the total number of T. rex dinosaurs you can spot.

T. rex

Facts about...

T. rex

Also known as Tyrannosaurus rex, it stood at 13ft (4m) tall and 40ft (12m) long, making it one of the most **ferocious beasts** that ever lived.

Barosaurus

Facts about...

Barosaurus

Standing at a massive 40ft (26m) long, Barosaurus was a plant-eating giant from the Jurassic period that used its **long tail** like a whip to fight back against attackers.

WRITE down the total number of Barosaurus dinosaurs you find.

Stegosaurus

WRITE down the total number of stegosaurus dinos you see.

Facts about...

Stegosaurus

The **bony plates** along its back look scary, but Stegosaurus only ate plants. That doesn't mean it couldn't put up a fight. Its massive **spiked tail** was deadly to any attacker.

Sticker gallery

Theropods
These meat-eaters were the deadly hunters of the dinosaur age.

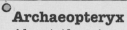

Pterodactylus
One of the best-known pterosaurs, it had a short neck and a long tail that helped it fly.

Archaeopteryx
About the size of a pigeon, Archaeopteryx was the first bird.

STICK the correct stickers for each frame in the right place.

Barapasaurus
Unlike most sauropods, Barapasaurus had sharp, sawlike teeth.

Nothosaurus
A fast, agile swimmer, this reptile hunted in the seas but could also walk on land.

COLOR
the scene and write a
description in the box.

Dinosaur life

Even though the world was a very different place when dinosaurs existed, in many ways dinosaurs had more in common with modern animals than you might think.

Don't forget to put your stickers in first.

Page _____

Page _____

FIND

these pictures on pages 36–49 and write the page numbers in the boxes.

Page _____

Page _____

Page _____

Page _____

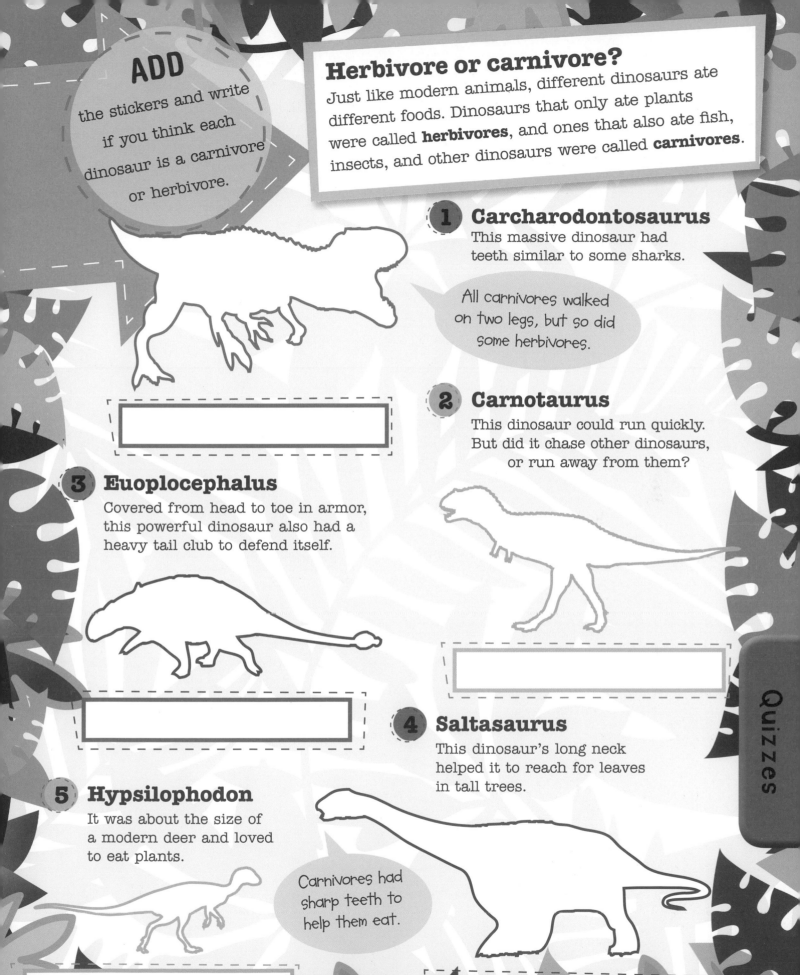

ADD

the stickers and write if you think each dinosaur is a carnivore or herbivore.

Herbivore or carnivore?

Just like modern animals, different dinosaurs ate different foods. Dinosaurs that only ate plants were called **herbivores**, and ones that also ate fish, insects, and other dinosaurs were called **carnivores**.

1 Carcharodontosaurus
This massive dinosaur had teeth similar to some sharks.

All carnivores walked on two legs, but so did some herbivores.

2 Carnotaurus
This dinosaur could run quickly. But did it chase other dinosaurs, or run away from them?

3 Euoplocephalus
Covered from head to toe in armor, this powerful dinosaur also had a heavy tail club to defend itself.

4 Saltasaurus
This dinosaur's long neck helped it to reach for leaves in tall trees.

5 Hypsilophodon
It was about the size of a modern deer and loved to eat plants.

Carnivores had sharp teeth to help them eat.

Quizzes

35

Who gets dinner?

Not all dinosaurs could defend themselves against attackers—and if they couldn't run away they would end up being another dinosaur's dinner!

FIND ☑

which path leads to the dinosaur in the middle and check the box.

Facts about...

Utahraptor

One of the deadliest dinosaurs of the Early Cretaceous, Utahraptor had a huge **hooked claw** on each of its hind feet that it used to attack its prey.

Facts about...

Iguanodon

Even though it was about the same size as an elephant, Iguanodon only had a sharp **thumblike spike** to defend itself from other dinosaurs.

END

Copy the SCENE

Are you a budding artist? By copying each square of the grid below, you'll be able to draw a great dinosaur scene in no time.

Which of these dinosaurs can you spot in the image?

Edmontonia

Triceratops

Diplodocus

T. rex

Pterodactylus

Stegosaurus

1 - - - - - - - - - - - - - - - - - -

2 - - - - - - - - - - - - - - - - - -

3 - - - - - - - - - - - - - - - - - -

4 - - - - - - - - - - - - - - - - - -

Home sweet home

Dinosaurs lived in different places, called habitats. There were six main types, and where a dinosaur lived depended on factors such as climate and the availability of food.

Mountains

Even though food was scarce here, dinosaur fossils have been found near mountains.

Forests

The trees in forests were a rich source of food for many plant-eaters.

Swampland

Swamps were perfect for both fish-eating and plant-eating dinosaurs.

I liked to be in wet areas with trees and fish.

There weren't that many plants where I lived.

I lived in a very hot, dry, and dusty place.

1

2

3

Spinosaurus lived in the...

Swampland

Plateosaurus lived in the...

Gallimimus lived in the...

Desert plains

The Earth was hotter than it is today, with vast deserts all over. Some dinosaurs adapted to life in the desert.

MATCH

each dinosaur to its habitat based on the clues given below.

Riverbanks

All living things need water to survive, so a lot of dinosaurs lived by rivers and coasts.

Add more dinosaurs to the scene using stickers.

Scrubland

Not too many plants grew here, but scrubland was home to many early dinosaurs.

My home was high up, by lots of rocks.

My habitat had plenty of water.

There were lots of tasty trees where I lived.

4

5

6

Edmontonia lived in the...

Herrerasaurus lived in the...

Stegosaurus lived in the...

41

Hunter and
hunted

For carnivores (meat-eaters), dinner was often another dinosaur—sometimes the dinosaur being eaten was a lot bigger than the dinosaurs eating it!

Deinonychus

This ferocious hunter from the Early Cretaceous is named "terrible claw," after the deadly claws on its feet.

CONNECT

the dots to reveal the rest of the picture, then color it in.

Games

Hunting

Facts about...

When taking on a bigger dinosaur, a group of smaller predators may have **ganged up** to attack it. Many modern animals, such as hyenas and wolves, hunt this way, too.

43

Save the eggs

A Maiasaura has been separated from her babies. Find objects to use as counters and help guide her back to her nest.

Start
Roll a die and move the correct number of steps along the board.

11

10
Egg fact
Some species of dinosaur sat on their nests in the same way chickens do.

9
A Brachiosaurus offers you a shortcut. **Go forward** to step 22.

8

12
You're being chased! Climb a vine to escape and **go back** to step 1.

13

14
You get slowed down by a passing herd. **Skip two** turns.

15

Finish

24
An Ankylosaurus is blocking your path. **Roll a six to end the game.**

44

1

2

3
Slide down the Barosaurus's neck. **Go forward** to step 19.

4
Hitch a ride on a Pterodactylus. On your next turn, **roll again.**

7
You hear a deadly T. rex nearby. **Go back** to step 2 and hide.

6

5

16
You take a break and feel rested. **Roll again**.

17
Egg fact
Scientists weren't 100 percent sure dinosaurs laid eggs. That is until 1920, when a fossilized nest was found in China.

18

19

23

22

21
You're almost crushed by a Barosaurus! **Skip a turn.**

20

What color were they?

As fossils (remains of prehistoric life) are made of stone, even experts can't be fully sure what color dinosaurs were. But by studying other animals we can get a few ideas.

COLOR in the dinosaurs. Read the facts to help you decide how to make them look.

Facts about...

Blending in

Some animals blend into the environment while hunting prey. A tiger's stripes keep it **hidden in tall grass**. Some dinosaurs may have been able to blend in, too.

Facts about...

Standing out

Peacocks and some other animals are colorful so they can **attract a mate** or threaten enemies. It's possible some dinosaurs also had ways of standing out.

Facts about...

Being plain

Animals such as elephants **don't have any predators**, so don't need to blend in or stand out. It's likely many dinosaurs were plain as well.

47

Sticker gallery

STICK the correct stickers for each frame in the right place.

Herds
Hadrosaurs and other dinosaurs often traveled in large herds.

Hunting
Some dinosaurs may have attacked in groups while hunting.

Eggs
Certain dinosaurs sat on their eggs the same way birds do.

Fishing
Baryonyx and other dinosaurs would stalk rivers looking for fish.

→ **COPY** the picture of the Baryonyx fishing and put a title on your drawing.

Studying dinosaurs

Experts called paleontologists dedicate their lives to studying fossils (the remains of prehistoric creatures) so that we can all learn more about these amazing creatures.

Page _____

Page _____

Page _____

Page _____

Page _____

Page _____

FIND these pictures on pages 52–64 and write the page numbers in the boxes.

Don't forget to put your stickers in first.

TEST

yourself to see how much you know about fossils. Don't forget to read the facts, too!

TRUE OR FALSE ?

1 The experts whose job it is to study fossils are called **dinologists?**

TRUE FALSE

2 "Sue," the T. rex fossil at the Field Museum, Chicago, cost the museum **$8.4 million** when it was bought in 1997.

TRUE FALSE

3 Fossils are **very common**, and you can buy them in most stores.

TRUE FALSE

4 In ancient China, dinosaur fossils were believed to be the remains of **dragons**.

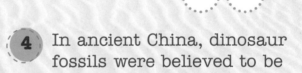
TRUE FALSE

5 The oldest fossils ever found are **1 billion years old**.

TRUE FALSE

6 **Teeth** are the most commonly found fossils.

TRUE FALSE

Plants

It's not just dinosaurs that become fossils. Plants and other animals do too.

Bones

In rare cases, entire skeletons are found preserved in rock.

Ammonites

Creatures from the ocean can also become fossils.

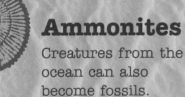

Footprints

Fossilized footprints give experts clues about how big dinosaurs were.

Quizzes

The great extinction

COLOR in the picture on the right side of the page.

Dinosaurs ruled the Earth for millions of years. But 65 million years ago, a giant meteorite struck the Earth causing them to become extinct.

How it happened

The meteorite struck the Earth with such force that it caused earthquakes, tsunamis, volcanic eruptions, and threw a cloud of dust into the sky, blocking the Sun.

"Extinct" means "no longer existing."

Are they all gone?

While dinosaurs as we think of them are all gone, modern birds are their direct descendents—making birds the only **surviving dinosaurs**!

Small mammals like this Nemegtbaatar survived.

Scientists think the meteorite was about 6 miles (10km) wide!

Facts about...

Survivors

No land animals bigger than a dog survived the mass extinction, but other animals such as fish, lizards, insects, and a few small mammals did.

How fossils are made...

It takes a very long time for fossils to form, and some of the earliest fossils are almost 3.5 billion years old!

COLOR

in the rest of the comic strip to complete the story of fossilization.

Fossilization

Living things can only become fossils if they are **buried quickly** after death. Otherwise, they simply decay and disappear. This is why fossils are so rare.

TRUE OR FALSE?
SEA CREATURES CAN'T BECOME FOSSILS.

70 million years ago...

1 A dinosaur dies and its body quickly sinks into thick mud, burying it and protecting it from the elements.

2 million years ago...

4 The Earth's plates shift again and a mountain range forms above the fossil.

54

Five years later...

2 Its flesh slowly rots away, leaving just the bones—which split apart and are buried under the ground.

50 million years ago...

3 The Earth's plates shift and a sea spreads over the area. Pressure makes the mud and sand harden.

Present day...

5 Over a long period of time, the mountains and other layers on top of the fossil are worn away by extreme weather. One day, a bone is spotted and paleontologists begin to dig up the pieces of the fossil.

Dinosaurs and their fossils

Fossils are the remains of things that lived long ago and that have been preserved in the Earth. Scientists study fossils to learn about prehistoric life.

Who am I?

Who am I?

Write the fossil letters heres.

A T. rex

B Deinonychus

Stone clues

Without fossils we would know very little about dinosaurs and prehistoric life. By **studying fossils**, scientists can find clues about a dinosaur's size, shape, diet, and more.

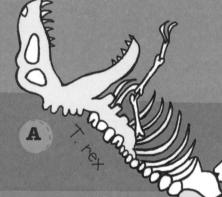

Fossil experts are called paleontologists.

Facts about...

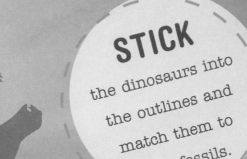

STICK
the dinosaurs into the outlines and match them to their fossils.

Who am I?

Who am I?

Match the stickers to these shapes.

Who am I?

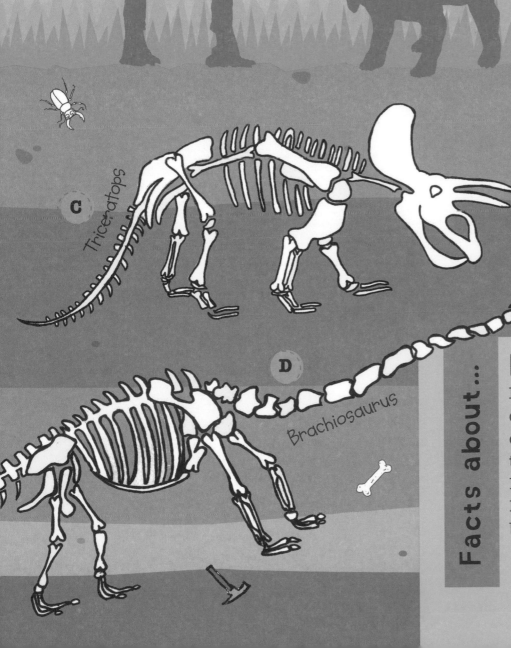

C

Triceratops

D

Brachiosaurus

E

Pterodactylus

Facts about...

Excavation

It can be a very long and difficult job to get fossils out of the ground because they can be stuck between layers of hard rock that has to be broken up bit by bit.

Draw your own
dinosaur

Drawing a dinosaur might seem hard, but it's not if you draw the dinosaur in steps. Start with this little Compsognathus.

Step 1

Begin by lightly copying the frame in pencil to work out how big your dinosaur will be. Add circles for the head, body, and limbs, as shown.

Step 2

Draw the outline of your dinosaur, using the circles as a guide. Don't worry about adding detail yet.

Step 3

Use an eraser to remove the guides. Add details such as claws, eyes, and teeth for the finishing touches. Finally, color it in!

I'm about the same size as a Compsognathus!

DRAW a Compsognathus in the space below. Don't forget to practice!

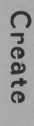

Facts about...

Compsognathus

One of the smallest predators ever was **Compsognathus (COMP-sog-NAITH-us)**, which was only about the size of a big chicken! Amazingly, despite its size, it could run at speeds up to a blazing 25mph (40kph)!

Dino dig notes

With so many species of dinosaur, pterosaur, and marine reptile, experts take notes to keep track of all the species. Add pictures to make the notes complete.

Piatnitzkysaurus
(PEA-at-NITS-key-SORE-us)

- **LENGTH:** Up to 13ft (4m)
- **FOUND IN:** Forests
- **FOOD:** Meat
- **LIVED:** Middle Jurassic

STICK
the stickers in the right place to finish the research. Use the shapes as a guide.

Albertosaurus
(al-BERT-oh-SORE-us)

- **LENGTH:** Up to 30ft (9m)
- **FOUND IN:** Forests
- **FOOD:** Meat
- **LIVED:** Late Cretaceous

Cryolophosaurus
(CRY-oh-loaf-oh-SORE-us)

- **LENGTH:** Up to 26ft (8m)
- **FOUND IN:** Plains
- **FOOD:** Meat
- **LIVED:** Early Jurassic

Mosasaurus
(MOSE-ah-SORE-us)

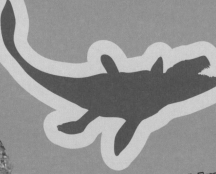

- **LENGTH:** Up to 50ft (15m)
- **FOUND IN:** Oceans
- **FOOD:** Fish, squid, shellfish
- **LIVED:** Late Cretaceous

Ouranosaurus
(ooh-RAN-uh-SORE-us)

- **LENGTH:** Up to 23ft (7m)
- **FOUND IN:** Desert plains
- **FOOD:** Plants
- **LIVED:** Early Cretaceous

Efraasia
(E-FRAHS-ee-A)

- **LENGTH:** Up to 23ft (7m)
- **FOUND IN:** Forests
- **FOOD:** Plants
- **LIVED:** Late Triassic

Heterodontosaurus
(HET-er-oh-DON-toe-SORE-us)

- **LENGTH:** Up to 3ft (1m)
- **FOUND IN:** Scrubland
- **FOOD:** Plants
- **LIVED:** Early Jurassic

Mamenchisaurus
(ma-MEN-chee-SORE-us)

- **LENGTH:** Up to 85ft (26m)
- **FOUND IN:** Forest plains
- **FOOD:** Plants
- **LIVED:** Late Jurassic

Elasmosaurus
(el-LAZZ-moe-SORE-us)

- **LENGTH:** Up to 45ft (14m)
- **FOUND IN:** Oceans
- **FOOD:** Fish, squid, shellfish
- **LIVED:** Late Cretaceous

Ichthyosaurus
(ICK-thee-oh-SORE-us)

- **LENGTH:** Up to 6ft (2m)
- **FOUND IN:** Oceans
- **FOOD:** Fish
- **LIVED:** Early Jurassic

fossil

STICK the missing pieces of the skeleton back on to fix the fossil.

Museums all over the world have amazing fossil collections you can visit. Seeing dinosaur skeletons up close gives you a much better idea of how big they were.

Parasaurolophus

Pronounced PA-ra-SORE-oh-LOAF-US, is famous for its **long, curved skull**, which it might have used like a trumpet to warn its herd of danger.

Parasaurolophus could walk on its hind legs or on all fours.

Parasaurolophus skeleton

Parasaurolophus

Which hadrosaur head is that?

1 Corythosaurus had a small snout with a rounded crest at the top of its head.

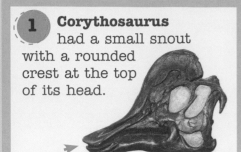

2 Lambeosaurus had a narrow mouth and a crest that resembled an ax blade.

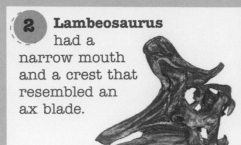

3 Brachylophosaurus had a deep snout and a rectangle-shaped skull that was flat on top.

Find the **STICKERS** that match the skulls.

All hadrosaurids had strong, stiff tails.

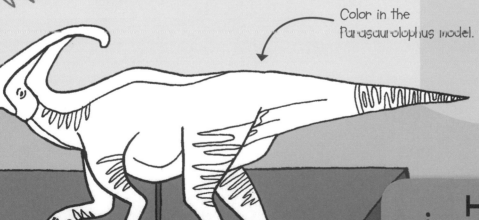

Color in the Parasaurolophus model.

Parasaurolophus model

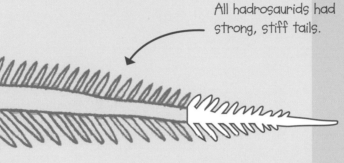

Facts about... Hadrosaurids

Parasaurolophus belonged to a group of dinosaur called hadrosaurids. This group of plant-eating dinosaur from the Late Cretaceous was famous for its strange head and **ducklike bill**.

63

Sticker gallery

STICK
the correct stickers for each frame in the right place.

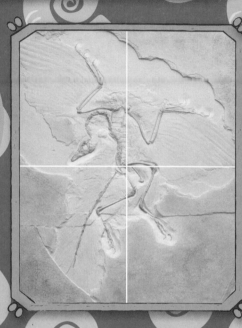

Teeth
The most commonly found fossils are usually teeth.

Feathers
Fossils like this show scientists that some dinosaurs had feathers.

Eggs
We know dinosaurs laid eggs because scientists have found their fossils.

Coprolites
The name for fossilized poop, these give us clues about a creature's diet.

Skulls
The size of a dinosaur's skull can help us figure out a dinosaur's size.

Use the colors as clues to where to place these dinosaurs on **page 8.**

Fill the scene on **pages 8–9** with these dinosaurs. Use the extras any way you like!

These stickers belong on **pages 12–13**.

Here are some extra stickers. Use them for decoration if you like.

Decorate the pages of the book with these!

Piece together these sticker puzzles on **page 16**.

These are extras for fun or decoration.

Stick these slippery sea monsters on **pages 24–25**.

Use these extra ones anywhere you like.

74

Solve this puzzling dinosaur jigsaw on **page 27**...

...And this one on **page 26**.

These stickers belong on **page 32**.

Stick these fearsome pterosaurs on **pages 20–21**.

Place these stickers on **page 32**.

Here are footprints and other extras to use as you like.

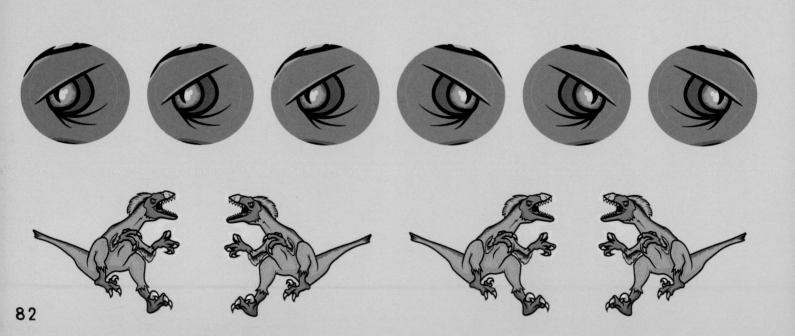

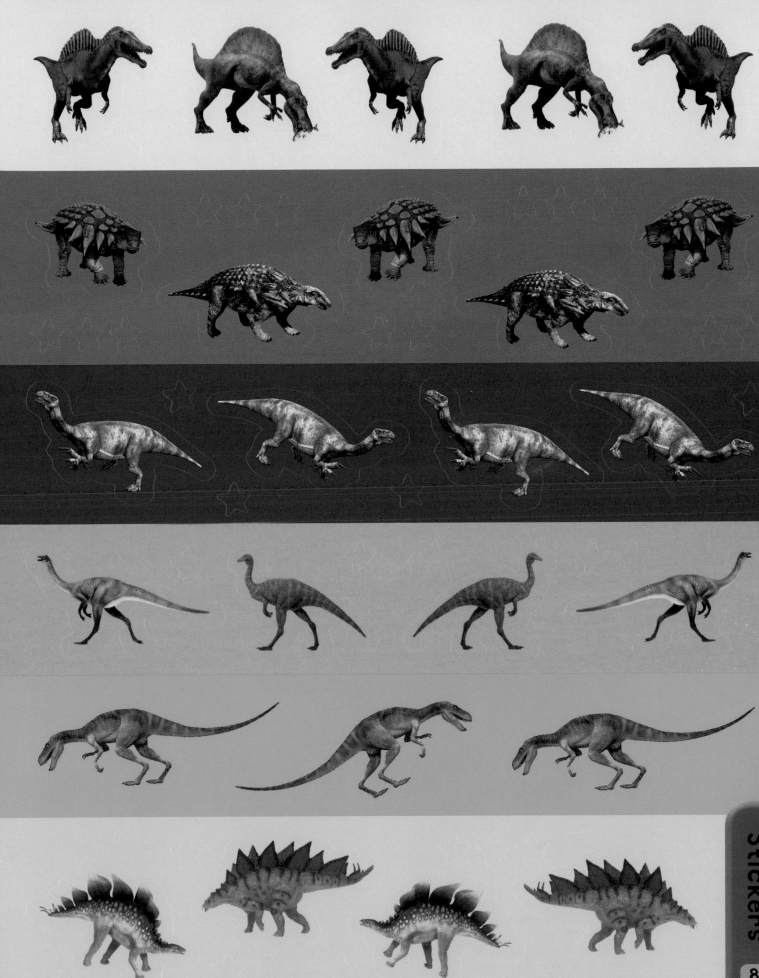

These footprints and skulls are spares to use wherever you like.

Place these stickers on **pages 56–57**.

Use these dino footprints anywhere you like.

Use these on **pages 62–63**. The bottom three are extras.

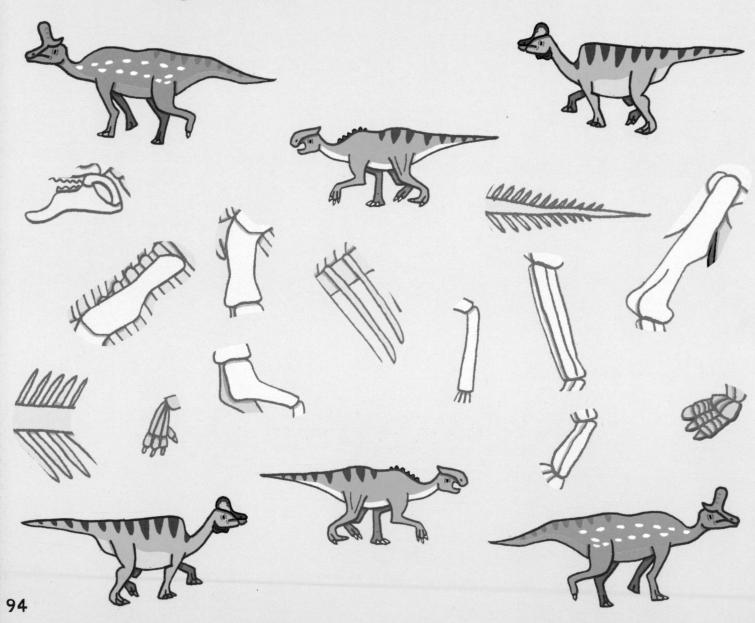

What will you do with these spare fossils?